I Get It!
I Get It!

How John Figures It Out

**One Boy's Journey and Triumph
with Auditory Processing Disorder**

Understanding is the first step toward success. Once you "get it" you can accomplish anything.

**620 Wheat Lane
Wood Dale, IL 60191 | USA
630.860.9700 | www.StoeltingCo.com**

Text copyright © 2012 by Loraine Alderman and Yvonne Capitelli

Illustration copyright © by Stoelting Company

All rights reserved. No part of this publication may be reproduced, stored in a retrieval system or transmitted in any form or by any means electronic, mechanical, digital, photocopy, recording or otherwise without prior written permission of the publisher and authors.

Any resemblance to actual people and events in this book of fiction is purely coincidental.

Published by Stoelting Company; Wood Dale, Illinois 60191
www.stoeltingco.com

Production by Quantum Advertising and Design
Art by Julia Klimas
Contribution to appendix by Lisa Arian

ISBN 978-0-9847380-0-7
First Edition
January 2012
Printed & bound in China

FOREWORD

Many children with learning and communication problems actually have unidentified Auditory Processing Deficits. These children struggle to understand what they hear. They typically have problems listening in noisy environments or acknowledging new and unfamiliar words. Children with APD often feel they are not smart enough to "get it," and as a result they often develop low self-esteem and get easily frustrated.

"I Get It! I Get It! How John Figures It Out," is about a child who feels frustrated and not smart. But, he is smart! He is struggling with a real problem, an Auditory Processing Disorder (APD). John is having difficulty in school and at home. He begins to give up and feel overwhelmed, frustrated, dumb and very confused. John feels that the adults in his life think he is inattentive and just not trying hard enough. What John learns in this story is that his listening problems have a name, APD. He learns that, with modifications and help, he can succeed. John realizes that he is not "dumb" but a child with a learning problem that he can overcome. Colorful and expressive illustrations bring to life John's journey from confusion to triumph of understanding, good self-esteem and "figuring it out." Included at the end of the story you will find a helpful Glossary Of Terms, Ways You Can Help Your Child At Home And In School and a Resources List.

This book is for children of all ages who think they "just don't get it" even though they are listening. They will see that, just like John, they can finally say, "I get it! I get it!"

—*Jay R. Lucker Ed.D., CC-A/SLP, FAAA*

To all children, especially the ones that think they're not smart enough–Believe in yourself, be determined to succeed and you too will figure it out! Be amazing in your own way. To my best friend Rose–Thank you for supporting my dreams. To my beautiful and smart Daria Rose–I love you more than the moon and all the stars in the sky! — Y.C.

To my son Andrew–For your courage and strength in dealing with APD and inspiring me and everyone who knows you. To my husband Bill–For always being there for me and believing in me. To all my family and friends who accept me for who I am, APD and all. — L.A.

It was Monday morning and John was in school sitting at his desk feeling very confused. He wondered why he often misunderstood what his teacher was saying and it made him feel sad and angry. He was also thinking about how his parents often get upset with him whenever they asked him to do things at home.

All he kept thinking was...

"I just don't get it!"
"I just don't get it!"

All of a sudden John's teacher, Mr. Thomas, asked the class a question. John was very happy that he knew the answer and quickly raised his hand.

When Mr. Thomas called on him, John explained that because people are all different, they choose to have different hairstyles. Suddenly, the entire class burst out laughing. John didn't understand what was so funny. His teacher explained that he was asking about different styles of chairs, not hair. John's face turned red and he was very embarrassed. He thought that the teacher was asking about hair styles. Now he could see why all the other children were laughing. He felt like jumping up and running out of the room.

That day, on on his walk home from school all he kept thinking was,

"I just don't get it!"
"I just don't get it!"

When John arrived home from school, his Mom could see he was very upset. She gave him a big hug and said, "Go put your backpack in your room, bring down your dirty laundry bag and walk the dog. When you are all done, come have some of these yummy chocolate chip cookies I made for you."

John smiled and ran upstairs to put his backpack on his bed and then took the dog out for a walk. He hurried back to the kitchen and sat down, ready to eat some delicious cookies.

"Where is your dirty laundry?" his Mom asked. "I didn't hear you say anything about my laundry," replied John. His Mom said, "Please go and get your laundry before you have your cookies."

John stood up feeling annoyed and went back to his room to get his laundry. All he kept thinking was

"I just don't get it!"
"I just don't get it!"

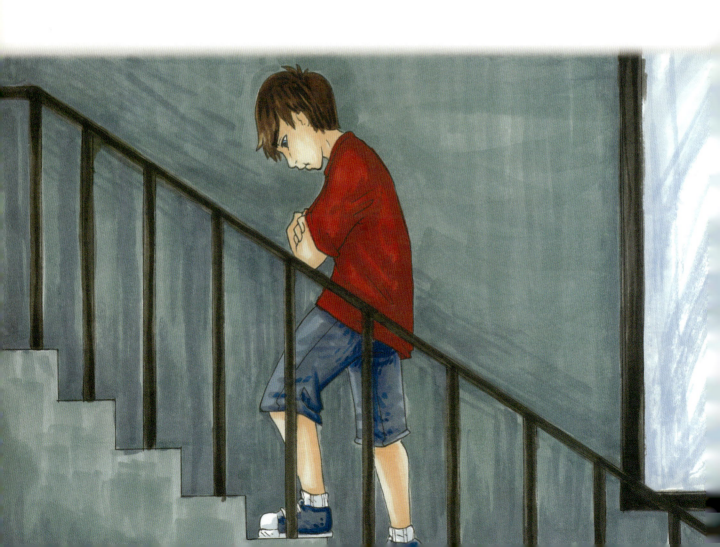

The next day in school while Mr. Thomas was teaching a math lesson, one of the boys in the back of the room was tapping his pencil on his desk, at the same time a girl sitting in front of John was popping her gum. As hard as John tried to listen to the words Mr. Thomas was saying, all John heard loud and clear was the popping of the gum and the tapping of the pencil. He missed many of the important words his teacher said and he became very frustrated and upset.

While walking home from school all he kept thinking was,

"I just don't get it!"
"I just don't get it!"
"I just don't get it!"

That night, John was determined to work very hard on the homework that his teacher told the class to do. He thought it seemed like more homework than usual because it took him more than two hours to finish. Even though he was annoyed that it took so long, he was happy and proud when he was done.

The next day at school, he was shocked when Mr. Thomas marked his homework incomplete. Mr. Thomas said that he completed the wrong pages in the book. "I told the class to do pages 1, 2 and 6 and not to do pages 3, 4 and 5."

John said, "I was almost sure you said to do pages, 3, 4, 5 and 6." Now he realized why it had taken him so long to finish his homework. He felt very frustrated and couldn't understand how he misunderstood the instructions. He went home feeling very upset, confused and angry. On his walk home, all he kept thinking was,

"I just don't get it"
      "I just don't get it"
            "I just don't get it"

That night at dinner John's Mom and Dad could see how sad he was. He told them everything that had been happening to him at school.

"I get so confused when Mr. Thomas tells the class what to do instead of writing it on the board, especially when he gives us the spelling words for the week. Whenever I hear noises during class, it drowns out what Mr. Thomas is saying. It's embarrassing when the other kids laugh at me. I also feel like you both get upset with me for not doing the things you ask me to do. I feel like no matter how hard I try,

"I just don't get it."

His Mom told him not to worry, that he was a smart boy and that she knew he was trying very hard to do his best. "Your Dad and I will speak to your teacher and together we will figure it out."

On Wednesday, John's parents met with his teacher. Mr. Thomas agreed that John seemed to be easily distracted by many background noises in the classroom that the other children didn't appear to notice. "He also misunderstands when I tell the class the assignments. John does very well on written tests some days, but not on other days."

Mr. Thomas suggested that they take John to an audiologist for testing. He thought it might explain why he is having such a hard time in school and at home.

A few days later, John and his parents met with Miss Brown, the audiologist. She told John that the tests would not make him uncomforable, that they would actually be fun, and not to be nervous. When he was finished, he could pick a snack from the jar.

Miss Brown had John wear a set of headphones. She explained that she would test his hearing and that he should raise his hand every time he heard a sound, first with his right ear and then with his left ear.

Then Miss Brown explained that John was going to hear a man's voice in the headphones. The voice was going to say some words or sentences and John should repeat exactly what he heard.

When they were done Miss Brown said, "You did a great job. Pick a snack out of the jar."

Later that week, John's parents met with Miss Brown to find out the results of John's tests. Miss Brown explained that John had something that was called APD, which stands for "Auditory Processing Disorder." It meant that John's ears were working fine, but that not all of the information that he heard was being understood correctly by his brain. Miss Brown said that it was like having a bad cell phone connection in which you missed some of the words completely or missed the beginning or ending of a word. She explained that her friend, Ms. Carmella, a speech therapist, could work with John to help him learn how to listen better and make it easier for him to understand what people were saying. She also suggested that they use a "Things To Do Chart" at home, so that John could easily read what and when he was supposed to do something.

Miss Brown told them all not to worry, that John would start to do better in school and at home after making some changes and working with Ms. Carmella. She said she would call John's teacher and explain what he could do to help John at school.

Miss Brown called John's teacher to discuss what was happening to John in class. Mr. Thomas was surprised to find out that noises in the classroom, like gum popping and pencil tapping, made it hard for John to hear the words that he was saying. John only heard the noises the students were making. Mr. Thomas said that from now on during class he would be more aware of when these noises happened so he could stop them. This way, John could hear what was being said.

Mr. Thomas told John that if a student was making a noise that bothered him, he should put his hand on his cheek. This would signal Mr. Thomas, without it seeming like John was tattling.

Every morning Mr. Thomas would write the homework assignment on the blackboard and post it on the classroom website. When John was at home, he could use the homework website to make sure he was doing the correct work.

John was also very happy that Mr. Thomas gave him extra time to finish his tests. To be sure John understood what he was supposed to do, Mr. Thomas read the directions and every question. John would then tell Mr. Thomas what he thought he was supposed to do. Mr. Thomas would then correct any misunderstandings before John took the test.

Another good idea that Miss Brown suggested, was for John to do homework with a friend from his class, in case he needed a little help.

John began to smile more and more. After only a few weeks of making changes and working with his speech therapist, Ms. Carmella, John started to see a big difference. He began to feel very happy. He was now completing all the correct homework assignments and his test grades were improving. After using the "Things To Do Chart," John and his parents were happier at home. It made it easier for him to understand what his Mom and Dad were asking him to do.

Sometimes, John still has a hard time, but he knows he is a smart boy and he feels much happier. He really likes how he has made some new friends at school.

John wishes he had talked to his parents sooner about his troubles. With the help of his parents, teacher, audiologist and speech therapist, John is doing much better at home and in school.

Now when John walks home from school, he has a huge smile on his face. All he keeps thinking is,

"I get it!"

"I get it!"

"I get it!!!"

GLOSSARY OF TERMS

Accommodations–Strategies and modifications used in the classroom for children with special needs. These accommodations allow the child to participate in academic or testing situations so they are on the same level with non-handicapped peers, e.g., allowing the child to have extra time for completing tests.

Audiologist–Professional with a state license to test hearing, dispense hearing aids and fit auditory systems to improve acuity or processing. Some audiologists also evaluate Auditory Processing Disorders.

Auditory Attention Problems–When a child has difficulty maintaining attention to auditorily-presented material, they do not understand to correctly complete tasks. These problems can be due to APD or attention problems such as Attention Deficit Disorder (ADD).

Auditory Fatigue or Overloading–Refers to a sense of feeling overwhelmed by too much information presented at one time. This may occur for some people with APD when the information being given is spoken quickly, and may involve unfamiliar vocabulary, as well as being presented in a noisy environment. This may occur when a teacher introduces a new lesson. The person with APD has to make a choice (usually done unconsciously) to either hold onto the information they have taken in at that point, and not take in any new information, or let go of the information that they have heard so far. The person with APD feels overwhelmed and reacts negatively on an emotional level. Auditory fatigue can also occur at the end of the day due to all the energy that has been expended trying to listen throughout the day.

Auditory Learning Disability–IDEA defines a specific learning disability as being related to a variety of factors. An auditory learning disability is a disorder in understanding spoken language, due to imperfect listening, that is not due to underlying hearing problems, language deficits, attention deficits or cognitive limitations. An auditory learning disability is a specific learning disability in which the individual has a problem understanding spoken language due to an Auditory Processing Disorder (APD).

Auditory Processing Disorder (APD)–A disruption in the processing of information, heard through the ears, because the brain does not correctly interpret sounds, phonemes and words or sentences that are heard. This has also been called Central Auditory Processing Disorder (CAPD), (Central) Auditory Processing ((C)APD), Auditory Perceptual Disorder and Auditory Processing Deficit.

Extended Time on Tests–An accommodation increasing the amount of time on a test, for a special needs student, beyond the time given to the other children within the classroom.

Frequencies of Sound–Sound travels through the ear in a series of waves or vibrations. The number of vibrations produced in one second is called the frequency of sound. The frequencies of hearing testing go from low frequencies (like voices only) of 250Hz to middle frequency sounds like vowels and some louder consonant sounds at 1000Hz to very, very high frequencies above speech sounds (such as the sounds of the piccolo at 8000Hz). Frequency is measured in Hertz (Hz).

FM Systems–A teacher speaks into a microphone attached to a transmitter that sends the teacher's voice to a receiver attached to a loudspeaker (called a sound field or classroom system) or headphones worn by the child (called an individual system). The teacher's voice is amplified above the background noise level to make the voice easier to hear. The headphones worn by the child will block out any background noise. FM systems are often recommended for children with APD, and are appropriate for those who fail the background noise test during the APD assessment.

Hearing–Refers to the sensory act of receiving and being aware of sound. Auditory acuity relates to the softest level a person can hear. This is also called, "hearing thresholds."
Hearing is assessed in two ways:
1. Air Conduction, in which sound enters the outer ear and travels through the middle ear to the inner ear stimulating the auditory nerve. The sound then travels to the brain where it is interpreted and auditory processing occurs.
2. Bone conduction, which is when the bones of the head are vibrated and sound travels directly to the inner ear, to the auditory nerve, and eventually to the brain.

Hearing Screening–Measurement of only certain frequencies and intensity levels assessed by air conduction. If a problem is found during a screening, a referral for a full hearing evaluation by an audiologist should be made.

Individualized Educational Plan (IEP)–Every child who has some type of impairment that affects learning can receive an Individual Educational Plan. This plan is created at a meeting attended by school personnel, parents and possibly the child. During this meeting, learning styles will be discussed as well as educational goals for optimum learning within the classroom. This plan falls under the umbrella of special education and is an outgrowth of the Individuals with Disabilities Education Act (IDEA).

Phonemes–The smallest units of individual sounds that are produced verbally. When combined, phonemes form words.

Phonemic Awareness–The ability to tell which phonemes one hears and to manipulate phonemes in words. It is an underlying auditory process required for reading, spelling, understanding new words and words spoken by people with accents.

Preferential Seating–An accommodation which allows the child ideal seating in the classroom to facilitate optimum learning.

Pre-Teaching–A strategy teachers use in the classroom for children to learn new information. It involves introducing any new vocabulary, unusual language use, and underlying concepts that link the terms to what the child already knows. This ensures that language does not interfere with concept acquisition and learning.

Section 504 of the ADA–This is the section of federal law, called the Americans with Disability Act that protects children who are not in special education but need accommodations and modifications to participate in school with their peers. For example, a child with APD who does not require an IEP but still requires modifications and accommodations for testing and/or classroom environment can be provided with a 504 plan. This plan would need to be renewed yearly.

Speech-Language Pathologist–State licensed professional who provides evaluations and remediation therapy in the areas of articulation, voice, rate and rhythm of speaking (such as stuttering) and language disorders. Speech-Language Pathologists also provide remedial services for children with APD.

WAYS YOU CAN HELP YOUR CHILD AT HOME AND IN SCHOOL

Strategies applied at home and at school can alleviate some of the problem behaviors associated with APD. The following are some suggestions:

1. Explain Auditory Processing Disorder to your child, using age-appropriate language.

2. Help your child to identify noises that are irritating or interfere with the ability to concentrate (the ticking of a clock, the hum of a machine, sounds from the T.V., other people speaking in the background, etc).

3. When giving instructions to your child make sure you:
   - Keep eye contact with him/her
   - Speak at a slower pace
   - Break down multi-step instructions into smaller units
   - Have your child repeat back to you what they are supposed to do, in the child's own words.

4. Provide downtime for your child, after school, before starting homework or chores.

5. Find things that your child is good at, and encourage those activities. Auditory Processing Disorder tends to be a killer of self-esteem and the child needs to feel good at something.

6. Yelling does not work with children who have an Auditory Processing Disorder. When you as the parent are feeling frustrated, realize that your child is feeling even more frustrated than you.

7. Some children with Auditory Processing Disorders have poor receptive and/or expressive language skills. Work on building these skills by:
   - Taking your child food shopping and labeling different categories (fruits, vegetables, canned goods, meats, etc.).
   - Let your child help with preparing meals. Describe what you are doing; stirring, frying, cracking eggs, pouring, measuring, chopping, etc.
   - Expand vocabulary by putting words to objects and activities that normally are not spoken.

8. Keep a calendar visually available for them to refer to for:
   - Homework and project assignments
   - Chores
   - Extra curricular activities

9. Consider private speech and language therapy. If the child only receives speech therapy within the school environment, he/she will miss three to four months of therapy due to vacations and days off from school.

10. Consider private tutoring to help pre-teach and review subjects that are difficult.

11. Depending on the type of the Auditory Processing Disorder and whether other disorders are involved, apply for accommodations either under Section 504 of the ADA or through IDEA with an Individualized Educational Plan (IEP). When special education support services (including speech-language therapy) are needed, the child usually requires an IEP.

12. Help your child to understand his or her accommodations and services so that he/she can inform you if they are not received.

13. Meet with your child's teacher(s) and explain to them your child's needs and how they can work best with your him/her.

14. To help your child be organized in school, use color coded folders, notebooks and book covers.

15. Have teachers write down homework assignments as opposed to giving oral instructions.

16. If your child is involved with religious instruction, explain to the instructor about your child's learning needs. His or her needs are no different in this environment than in regular classroom environment.

17. Consider some of the following classroom/testing accommodations depending upon your child's needs:
    - Preferential seating
    - An extra set of textbooks to keep at home
    - Use of an FM System
    - Questions on tests to be re-read
    - Instructions/directions on tests to be re-read
    - Extended time on tests
    - Small group testing in an environment with minimal distractions
    - Have him/her paraphrase to check for understanding of instructions

RESOURCES

American Academy of Audiology (AAA)
11730 Plaza America Drive, Suite 300
Reston, VA 20190
800-222-2336

American Speech-Language-Hearing Association (ASHA)
2200 Research Boulevard
Rockville, MD 20850-3289
800-638-8255
www.asha.org

Auditory Processing Disorders in the United Kingdom (APDUK)
www.apduk.org

Educational Audiology Association (EAA)
3030 West 81st Avenue
West Minster, CO 80031
800-460-7322
www.edaud.org

National Coalition on Auditory Processing Disorders, Inc. (NCAPD)
www.ncapd.org

National Institute on Deafness and Other Communication Disorders
National Institutes of Health
31 Center Drive, MSC 2320
Bethesda, MD 20892-2320
nidcdinfo@nidcd.nih.gov

DR. LORAINE ALDERMAN is a licensed clinical psychologist and a certified school psychologist. She works in the New York City school system as a school psychologist, and has a private practice. Her first book *Don't You Get It? Living With Auditory Learning Disabilities* has sold worldwide. Dr. Alderman's focus is to advocate for children and adolescents with learning disabilities. She, as well as her father and son, have been diagnosed with Auditory Processing Disorder. Dr. Alderman was voted Best Psychologist by the readers of the Long Island Press for 2007, 2008 and 2011. (www.psychdocinfo.com)

YVONNE CAPITELLI first fell in love with writing as a young child growing up on Long Island, NY. She is an award-winning author, and children's motivational speaker, who focuses on character building in an educational and fun way. She credits her daughter, Daria, for inspiring her to make her dream of being an author come true. Her first book and five-time award winner, *Daria Rose and The Day She Chose,* inspires children to take control of their lives by making good choices. Her passion is to encourage children to realize they hold the power to create a happy and successful life. She recently received the Literary Classics Gold Award. (www.dariarosebooks.com)